ANTONIO BROWN

SUPERSTAR WIDE RECEIVER

BIG BUDDY NFL SUPERSTARS

Big Buddy Books
An Imprint of Abdo Publishing
abdobooks.com

DENNIS ST. SAUVER

abdobooks.com

Published by Abdo Publishing, a division of ABDO, PO Box 398166, Minneapolis, Minnesota 55439.

Big Buddy Books™ is a trademark and logo of Abdo Publishing.

Printed in the United States of America, North Mankato, Minnesota.
052019
092019

Cover Photo: efks/Getty Images; Getty Images.
Interior Photos: Andy Lyons/Getty Images (p. 9); Ben Liebenberg/AP Images (p. 11); Ben Margot/AP Images (p. 29); Gene J. Puskar/AP Images (p. 23); Gregory Shamus/Getty Images (p. 13); Jared Wickerham/Getty Images (p. 21); Jason Merritt/Getty Images (p. 25); Justin K. Aller/Getty Images (pp. 5, 27); Karl Walter/Getty Images (p. 15); Kevork Djansezian/Getty Images (p. 19); Rob Carr/Getty Images (p. 17).

Coordinating Series Editor: Elizabeth Andrews
Graphic Design: Jenny Christensen, Cody Laberda

Library of Congress Control Number: 2018967163

Publisher's Cataloging-in-Publication Data

Names: St. Sauver, Dennis, author.
Title: Antonio Brown: superstar wide receiver / by Dennis St. Sauver
Other title: Superstar wide receiver
Description: Minneapolis, Minnesota : Abdo Publishing, 2020 | Series: NFL superstars | Includes online resources and index.
Identifiers: ISBN 9781532119804 (lib. bdg.) | ISBN 9781532174568 (ebook)
Subjects: Brown, Antonio, 1988- --Juvenile literature. | Football players--United States--Biography--Juvenile literature. | Wide receivers (Football)--Juvenile literature. | Pittsburgh Steelers (Football team)--Juvenile literature.
Classification: DDC 796.3326409 [B]--dc23

CONTENTS

SUPERSTAR WIDE RECEIVER

Antonio Brown is a star player in the National Football League (NFL). He is a wide receiver for the Oakland Raiders in California.

Antonio played for the Pittsburgh Steelers in Pennsylvania for nine seasons. In 2019, he left the Steelers to join the Raiders.

SNAPSHOT

NAME:
Antonio Tavaris Brown Sr.

BIRTHDAY:
July 10, 1988

BIRTHPLACE:
Miami, Florida

POSITION:
Wide Receiver

COLLEGE TEAM:
Central Michigan University Chippewas

PAST NFL TEAM:
Pittsburgh Steelers

CURRENT TEAM:
Oakland Raiders

EARLY YEARS

Antonio's father Eddie was a star player for the Arena Football League. His younger brother Desmond also played football.

Antonio went to Miami Norland High School. There, he starred in football and track. In football, he played quarterback, wide receiver, running back, and punt returner!

DID YOU KNOW?

Antonio is friends with Dwayne "The Rock" Johnson. He and The Rock work out with the same trainer.

Where was Antonio Brown born?

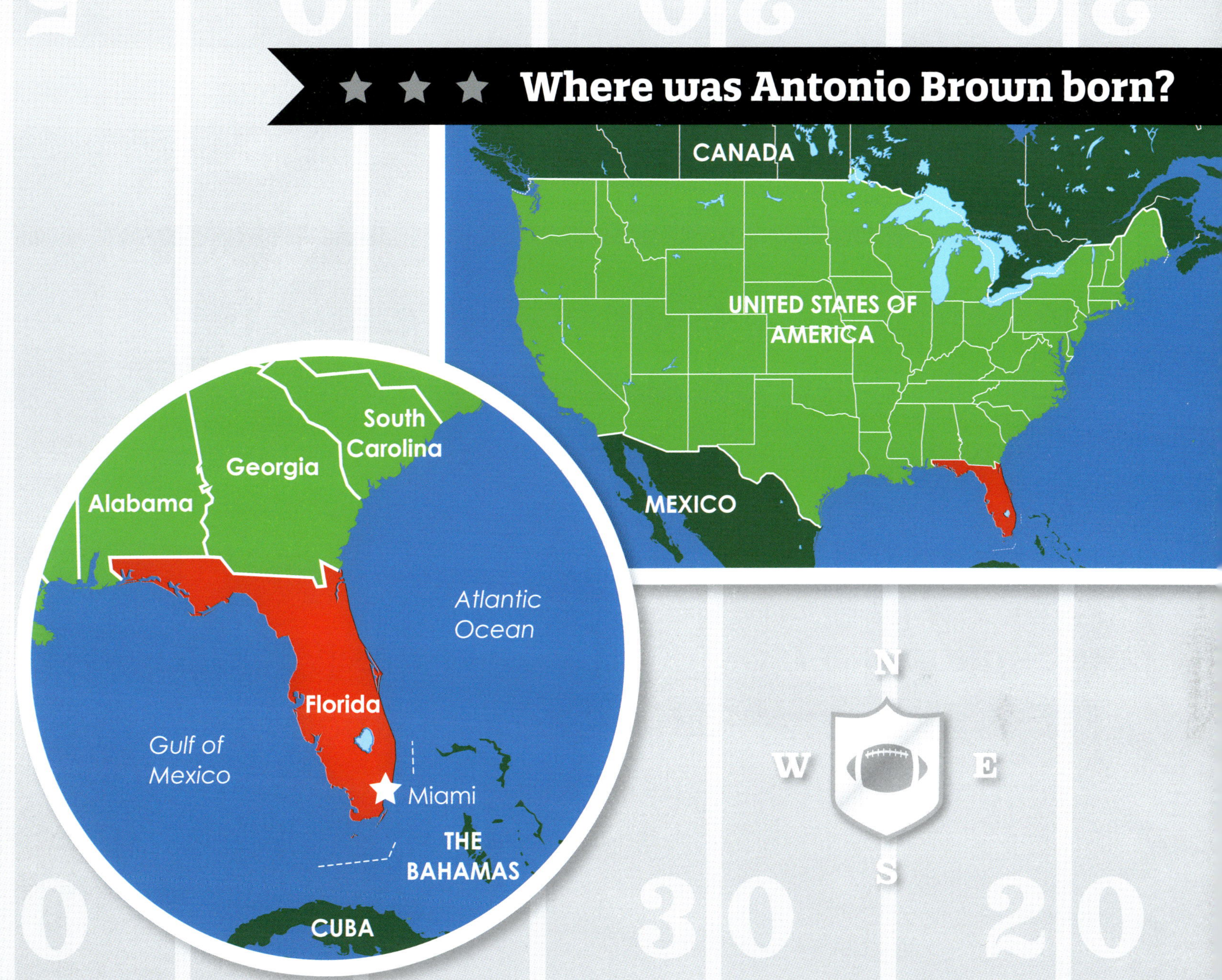

STARTING OUT

In 2007, Antonio attended Central Michigan University. After only a few weeks of play, he earned a **scholarship** to continue playing as wide receiver.

In his freshman year, Antonio had 102 **receptions** for more than 1,000 yards (914 m). For his efforts, he earned the Mid-American **Conference** Freshman of the Year Award.

The University of Central Michigan Chippewas team plays in the Mid-American Conference in the West Division.

In his second year of college in 2008, Antonio started each game of the season. The following season, he set a personal record with 13 **receptions** for 178 yards (163 m) in a single game.

He finished his college **career** after three seasons. By the end, he had caught 305 **passes** for 22 touchdowns. He impressed his coaches and NFL **scouts**.

At five-feet, ten-inches (178 cm) tall, coaches worried that Antonio was too small to play in the NFL. But he showed his skill during the 2010 NFL Draft workouts.

BIG DREAMS

In 2010, Antonio left college before his senior year. He wanted to become a **professional** football player.

The Pittsburgh Steelers selected him in the NFL **draft**. He was the twenty-second wide receiver to be chosen. For being chosen so low, he surprised everyone with his **incredible** skills.

Antonio was 22 years old when he began playing with the Steelers. He played in only nine games his first year.

GOING PRO

In Antonio's first season with the Steelers, he helped the team to the Super Bowl. The Steelers lost to the Green Bay Packers, but he had a very successful year.

In 2011, Antonio became the first player to have more than 1,000 yards (914 m) receiving and returning in the same season. So he was selected as a punt returner for that season's **Pro Bowl**.

In 2013, Antonio broke another NFL record. He had at least five catches and 50 yards (46 m) in each game of the season.

During the 2013 season, Antonio became the second Steelers player to catch 100 **passes** in a season. His teammates said that he has great hands. That means he can catch almost anything thrown his way.

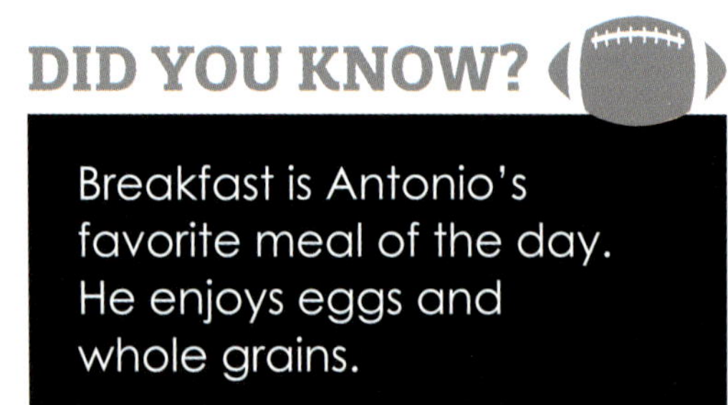

Antonio helped the Steelers make it to the playoffs six times in nine years.

A RISING STAR

Antonio continued to improve each year. In 2014, he led the league with 1,698 receiving yards (1,553 m). That season, he was named **First Team All-Pro**.

The wide receiver was named First Team All-Pro for the next three seasons as well. In 2017, he led the league again with 1,533 receiving yards (1,402 m).

Antonio presented an award at ESPN's 2018 ESPY Awards. He and Alex Morgan *(right)* handed out the prize for Best Olympic Moment.

Antonio kept setting records for the Steelers. He is fourth in NFL history for most receiving yards in a single season. In 2015, he had 1,834 receiving yards (1,677 m)!

That same year, he became the first player with at least 125 **receptions** for two straight seasons. He was also the first with at least 100 receptions five years in a row.

The Steelers made it to the wild card round for the 2014 season. The next season, Antonio set a career record with 136 receptions.

OFF THE FIELD

Antonio has five children. His sons are named Antonio Jr., Autonomy, Ali, and Apollo. His daughter's name is Antanyiah.

In 2016, Antonio appeared on the ABC dance **competition** show *Dancing with the Stars*. Three years later, he was in Drake's music video for the song "God's Plan."

When he was with the Steelers, Antonio drove a black and yellow Rolls Royce.

GIVING BACK

Antonio **supported** the Children's Hospital of Pittsburgh with his time and money. He hosted a **charity** softball game to raise money for the cause.

In 2016, Antonio gave $100,000 to the Children's Hospital. The money helped support sick children during their stay.

Antonio worked with the Pittsburgh Food Bank to pack and give away 5,000 bowls of soup.

AWARDS

Antonio has set many records for the Steelers and the NFL. He has also won several awards like 2016 Fantasy Player of the Year.

The wide receiver has appeared in seven **Pro Bowl** games since 2011. He has also been one of the NFL's Top 100 players five times. In 2018, he was number two on the Top 100 players list.

Antonio threw a touchdown pass during an NFL game in 2014! It is usually the quarterback who throws touchdown passes.

BUZZ

Since joining the NFL in 2010, Antonio led the Steelers to many wins. Now he is excited to lead the Raiders to victory. Fans cannot wait to see what Antonio does next!

DID YOU KNOW?

Antonio likes to start new projects to keep busy. In 2019, he was on the cover of the *Madden NFL 19* video game.

Raiders general manager Mike Mayock (*right*) welcomed Antonio to the team in March 2019.

GLOSSARY

career a period of time spent in a certain job.

charity (cher-UH-tee) a group or a fund that helps people in need.

competition (kahm-puh-TIH-shuhn) a contest between two or more persons or groups.

conference a group of sports teams that play against each other and that are part of a larger league of teams.

draft a system for professional sports teams to choose new players.

First Team All-Pro an honor given to the most outstanding players in the NFL at each position.

incredible (in-KREH-duh-buhl) extremely or amazingly good, great, or large.

pass to throw the football in the direction of the opponent's goal.

Pro Bowl a game that features the best players in the NFL. It does not count toward regular-season records.

professional (pruh-FEHSH-nuhl) paid to do a sport or activity.

reception the act of catching a pass thrown toward the opponent's goal.

scholarship (SKAH-luhr-ship) money or aid given to help a student continue his or her studies.

scout a person whose job is to search for talented performers or athletes.

support to provide help or encouragement to.

ONLINE RESOURCES

To learn more about Antonio Brown, please visit **abdobooklinks.com** or scan this QR code. These links are routinely monitored and updated to provide the most current information available.

★ ★ ★ INDEX ★ ★ ★